Turning the Lights Back On

Turning the Lights Back On

Poems by

Rebecca A. Spears

Cover design by Shay Culligan
Cover image by Rudy Issa on Unsplash
Author photo by Denise McDonald, 2025

ISBN: 979-8-90146-718-3

Kelsay Books
502 South 1040 East, A-119
American Fork, Utah 84003
Kelsaybooks.com

For Lena, Seth, and Riley

There is love answering to love, always

Acknowledgments

Thank you to the following publications, in which versions of these poems previously appeared:

B O D Y: "Madonna Wedding Ensemble"
Concho River Review: "Near Dusk"
Equinox Biannual Journal: "Turning the Lights Back On"
Four Corners: "Body Wishes," "Edge of the Bed"
The Nature of Our Times: America's Land, Water, Wildlife, and Other Natural Wonders (Paloma Press): "Allow Me, Unquestioned"
The Orchards Poetry Journal: "The Claim"
Persimmon Tree: "Luna Dance"
Reformed Journal: "Mirabilia, in the Garden," "There Was, and Is"
Waxing and Waning: "Between Dawn and Day, What Distance," "Roberto Capucci's *Angel d'Oro*"
Willawaw Journal: "The Migratory Seasons"
Willows Wept Review: "First, You Have to Know Darkness"

Gratitude to David Meischen, John McDermott, Margo Davis, Priscilla Frake, Sandi Stromberg, and Stan Crawford. Thanks also to Sasha West, cherished mentor and friend. And for my family and friends who share their lives with me and even tolerate my poetry, I love you.

Contents

Turning the Lights Back On

On that day when you meet
yourself at the gate
and slip into the world again,

there, your eyes stripped
of their usual expectations
will focus on the finest point

of light ahead as you settle into
the thrall of a long walk—

this, after you've escaped from
the funk that slugged you silly,
leaving you a carcass of yourself—

this, after the fictions and nonfictions
ceased their competing narratives

and you ended your argument
with the world (clarity is its own
best argument, after all)—

you could allow yourself
to become the still-point once more,

knowing again how to move
in all directions, and with good will,
find a way back to the crowds or

go north to the green pond, cypress
shadows, the chirping frogs.

Even now, this story is a part of the mending.
Mending is a thing that continues.

—Katherine Larson, *Wedding of the Foxes*

Body Wishes

I could live without many objects, even
this bowl on my writing desk, a small perfect
thing etched with trees, glazed cream
for sky. Though I give into it, imagine
the kiln firing—and being contained—
I could live without it surely.

My friend tells me my need to be held
is just what I should not want. Tells me I
ought to leave my love, return to my own
body, reclaim what was mine and plow
my solitude back into the land.

I know how a flood overtakes
and makes the alluvial plains fertile.
A body pregnant soaks the sheets before
the new life. And I would be flooded,
couldn't remain or be turned aside
or let even loss hold me.

Edge of the Bed

I have lain in the dark alone every night for too long.
At times I hear someone get up to leave—
someone disinterested—

though really, I've shared this bed with no man
but you. Often I curl into the impression
you left here

or wake to see you at the bed's edge, dark head down,
open palms anchored on the mattress.
It is daylight

or at least it is in this dream that goes on all night.
Sometimes we are contained in a vessel
on a cobalt sea.

Then comes midnight and you at the rail, with plans
to disappear and begin again. This dream
I keep harboring.

I wake always facing the empty side, rise quickly
to pull the comforter taut. Nothing's changed
that way.

The Bell Founder Advises Me

Some days, you may appear stock still,
he says, but your mind is humming
like a standing wave, ready to let loose,
as the longitudinal sound that would
spiral around a bell's perimeter from its top
to the ever-widening bow, its mouth
opening with hunger for the complex
chord of a perfectly tuned body.

(I think, even if I seem half-deaf of late,
the timbre, the standing waves set free,
want to resonate through me, remind
me to live, to freefall with the sounds,
imagine whatever life is left in me
chiming in, making pleasurable pitches,
melodic harmonics, the layering of
the root note, the third, the fifth.)

And the air it travels through, he says,
is made clearer whether it rings out
a celebration or call to attention,
to return to your origins filled with vision
just as a bell will have its own genius
set in the bronze alloy when it is heated
to a radiant liquid, allowing the heart
and soul to enter its body and rest there.

Allow Me, Unquestioned

In the bee-loud glade . . .
peace comes dropping slow.
—W. B. Yeats

Permit me to approach
my bee boxes
only lighting the smoker.

Let me remove the veil
and gloves, the waxed coat,
kick off the bog boots.
Let smoke turban my head
and curl down my arms.

Allow me to reach into the combs,
unquestioned.

I invite the honeybees to swarm me.
I want to wear them all day, revel
in the brocade
of their glitter and sting.

See how the honey
combs my porous bones,
straightens my unstable spine.
I've become statuesque,
prismatic.

Bee balm paints
my eyes, amber colors
my focus. Dressed as I am,
I traipse the wild indigo
to find my way farther into
the swarming glade.

History from the Body

When we first stepped from dark to light,
didn't we know the design of all life
instinctively? The body told us

a dry throat meant *water,*
feeling low or faint meant *salt,*
gooseflesh asked for *fire* and *fur.*

Later the body found it needed *bitter*—
not all the time, sometimes. Derived
from zinc and copper, from soil.

The animal required minerals, though
it had no word for *need.* It wanted
what it needed—bitter for balancing

a honeyed tongue, after we'd emptied
the beehives. Cold springs for thirst
after devouring rabbits' flesh. The body

seemed satisfied. Except for a longing—
it became a signal fire. Early on
we recognized it and found a mate,

steadfast companion. The body showed us
how. And the children that came filled any
void after their ripping births.

Still, life was never *sour,* was it?
We could remember the sun after
every cold, dark storm, a lush valley

on the windward side of the hills,
the roasted joint of lesser animals,
savory in our mouths, long in our bodies.

Mirabilia, in the Garden

If, at the harvest, I bring you a jug of cold water,
and you drink till you are drunk, I am your servant.

If, in the late garden, I dig up roots and you coax a fire
from a rock, we shall become the feast.

Later, as frost scatters across the field like ashes
and crunches underfoot, I'll know it is you.

If the sun hits the red fox on the path, carving
a shadow beneath it, I will be struck blind for you.

Or when the running creek smooths itself over stones,
we'll join together, moss drooping from trees.

And when the eyes burn the object of your gaze,
let this world slip into a bank of snow-clouds.

Suppose darkening thoughts douse us like rain.
Your eyes will lead us like lanterns to shelter.

And if the cause of our joy is simply this turn
of the seasons, it's the hearth in which we're forged.

Roberto Capucci's *Angel d'Oro*

—Metropolitan Museum of Art

Her demeanor from a side angle
is unassuming, the Angel d'Oro
in pleated panels of gold and rose.
You can nearly hear the swishing
of silk taffeta as she tries to pass by
without disturbing you, though
isn't that what angels exist for—
to trouble us—*are we good enough,*

faultless enough, fair in our deeds?
Isn't that what the man who dressed her
was thinking as he pleated those wings?

This angel has appeared in sundry iterations
and a myriad of colors. In another venue
—Christie's—her dresser showed us a face
wrapped with white fabric, hooding
the woman. A bun-like knot in the back
secured the hood. I held my breath,
couldn't breathe, trapped like
that—with no eyes to see how he
had dressed me or what would happen
next. I couldn't bear it. I watch myself
unnerved, tearing through the fabric.

No Ordinary Time

Not easy to pigeonhole
after the children moved on
and my husband   (first
my husband)
I'd hold our dog
walk into and out of
every room in the house
knowing how a heart's chambers
fill momentarily then   empty

I devoted myself to this routine each day
before work   sleep
checking every quarter-hour
as I'd once followed phone calls
nosed open e-mail   unfolded
letterhead as if
there might be meaning in there
clots of meaning
from a believable witness
or some reason to imagine
a different conclusion

On summer evenings the dog
at the back door nuzzled
my hand   in the yard with her
the crazed mockingbirds grew
louder   heat-exhausted
famished   *aw aw aw*
the awful birds branched above
the garage   the sounds'
rough edges wearing me down.

Madonna Wedding Ensemble, House of Dior

—Metropolitan Museum of Art

Before the mute mannequin, I am
dumb-drunk. Before the mannequin,
with the stone-white face, downcast eyes,
I have lost my voice, like her, only
for me, it is momentary. You might

notice that her face twins
her sister-mannequins close by—
oh, there are so many of them.
And she—a snowfall of white tulle,
white silk—is angel, angelic*, ankiladq*

angelique, der Engel, engelgleich.
What disturbs me, and might trouble you,
is that vague expression. Distant, it shows
disinterest. Up-close it turns to something
like grief. Galliano of Dior has dressed her.

Her religion has dressed her. I can
nearly smell the censer and the incense.
Love among unequals is not a math problem.
Is more profane than sacred. It means
a woman available, without joy.

Across the way, an alabaster mourner
by Pere Ollet grieves, and I do too.
This woman-mannequin-angel-bride
exists to seduce, enchant, elevate us,
embroider us with faith in antique hierarchy.

Though plain cloth might do, these swaths
of threaded snow, the heavy head-dress
of gold cross and shooting stars—they make
the old grief she carries shine so irresistibly
that the woman recedes into stone.

Luna Dance

Last night, the Luna Moth,
          a chartreuse fluttering
beat against the window, attracted to
the saffron light
    of my reading lamp.

I thought she would beat herself to death
the way an anorexic refuses the universe
and the laws of physics.
                                        I turned on
the porch light to draw her away from
the window, and watched her fly
          a crazy circuit around my porch

finally settling on the deck-edge
before flying off into dark woods

perhaps attracted to fireflies along
the creek bed.
                        For a while, before I fell
asleep, I could think only of the creature's
greens—limes, willows, verdigris.

And in my sleep, Degas' Swaying Dancer,
her green skirt—so
          beautifully unreal.

An eclipse of moths
behind her fluttered like a corps
of thin, hungry dancers, their costumes
                                        full and fanciful—
a whirl of girls that flew
on a strong night breeze into the dark.

I don’t know how they survive.

Wounded Angel

—After the painting by Hugo Simberg

Two boys carry this drooping angel
along a path beside a silver bay.

Her robes hang loosely, freedom for gliding—
or tumbling?—from heaven to earth.

Grey clouds filter the sun's frail
light onto her wings tinged rust-red.

Her eyes are loosely bandaged,
as if any light would send her reeling.

The snowdrops she's holding—a sign
of early spring—surely the boys plucked them

for her. And what are the boys thinking?
What do they want? Were they taught

lessons in care and concern? Will other
boys mock them, catcall the angel?

I want to believe in these boys and what
they carry, the unreal weight of their task.

Who prizes the flat surface

or admires the caved-in stomach?
Who, in fact, worships such punishment?

And what does that mean, to empty
the body as if

we are offering hosannas, laying
palm fronds on a cold, stone altar?

A body might want plump curves,
but the mind can refuse, instead

torturing it—the torment of refusing,
the outsize thrill of outlasting hunger.

But, really, I haven't got that quite right,
now have I?

I'll try again—

In the emptied body, what other longing
could there be

except a hunger for the hands that fed
us first and loved us?

Or the hands that want us now, finding us
in both darkness and light.

Or the child issued to us in the shock
of lightning.

The empty body, and its unforgiving angles,
will starve itself to be fed with love.

Alterations

The seamstress wants you to empty
yourself before the pins go in.

You take no food for days,
hollow yourself, to be readied

and shaped from the outside in,
stealing yourself from yourself.

Yet you begin eating your distress,
afflicted, taking in more suffering

than you should. The seamstress must
let out the seams, tear into hems,

unstitch darts, remove rare
lace and such. Now you know for sure

you're heavy with hurt and ache.
You learn that no one sees you anymore.

Invisible, inflated—that's you. A balloon
high above, away from the crowds.

You want help. You want the secure
hand of anyone. Instead, poking

fingers find your ribs. Jibes
from the seamstress, laughter—

all in fun. Sighs and sneers,
the expense to cover you now.

Blue Roses

conjure the malformed and beautiful.

Think Laura, in *The Glass Menagerie,*
overly shy, dragging her leg, and

Jim calling her 'Blue Roses,' not knowing
pleurosis, really, yet aware of
her fragile allure.

So often the misshapen gathers
more interest than
perfection. An irregular thing

catches the eye, pulls the imagination
toward new perspectives.

I've remembered Laura
and Blue Roses so long.

So seemingly weak, she
dresses in pink and lavender-

blue—an exhausted flower,
with the beguiling symmetry
of compensating.

Sometimes I am right there with her
in a long-ago memory—
dragging my own leg
in its brace.

This vision
delicate as a glass figure
dislocates me

to nights my mother soothed
my aching legs until I
fell into sleep,

dreaming—my mother
smoothing her hands across
a length of polished cotton—

a white field, swirled with
watery blue roses,
emerald leaves,

impressionistic and uneven—
they were nearly disfigured.

And my mother,
delight overtaking her,
describing the dress
she would sew.

Arrested, I fell in love with
all the possibilities

of elegant defect and
beautiful chance.

Bowing into the Wind

Who interprets the world?
—Marie Howe

Really, I'm asking, *Who can we turn to?*
Cold rinses the fields, the mind.
The slow river breathes as we do

and on the levee tracks, the trains
follow, churning black smoke, with
slick rails guiding them on their way.

As my mother's arms. Steadied me
when I became a wife widowed early
by withering notions of love.

For three long years, bowing into the wind,
I wandered darkly through glacial nights
thinking I'd lost my bearings until

that night the distant lamps signaled
the windows of a home I knew,
a string of bells on the unlocked door.

The one person looking for me—
my mother, calling my name
into the cold-darkness.

I left my blue shrouds in shreds
at the threshold.

Mulberry Silk, Tussah Silk

You wander the fabric shop aisles; clerks
impatient, wonder if you'll ever buy a length.

The smoothest silk from the *Bombyx mori,*
the domesticated moth helpless, unable to fly.

Really, isn't that more beastly than knowing
the wild *Bombyx mandarina* ranged haphazardly

through oak trees, alighting on leaves
they want before spinning their cocoons?—

cocoons that will make the tussah, the *kosa.*
Its colors—you must wait to discover

while mulberry silk from the *Bombyx mori*
will be richly dyed any color you can imagine.

You must wonder about the single thread—
300 to 900 meters long—that can be unwound

from one domestic cocoon. Or the threads
cut short when the wild ones emerge and chew

through the cocoons. How they are spun
I cannot tell you. But the nubby shantungs

are gold-colored or cream, even dark brown
or coppery—it depends on the oak leaves

the moths feasted on. Isn't it more of an art
to see which color will emerge in one season

and not in another, to discover the nature
of the cloth you will get? Isn't the not-knowing

more fertile ground than overseeing all variables,
knowing beforehand the long and pure threads?

Choosing

I'm between two choices, or three,
a Liberty cotton, a nubby silk, paisley rayon,
each entirely perfect.

Which texture pleases me more?
Which color looks best? But what else
to choose except what's on sale—

even so, among the yards marked down,
do I choose loud or soft colors? prints
or solids? heavy fabric or lightweight?

I was once between wanting to end it
and not end it with you. For a long time
I knew I should. Why you wanted me

to rescue you or attempt to, I don't know.
But I knew you were one wild moth
feeding on oak leaves, who would fly off

to find a better feast, and me left longing
for your exquisite mind, your rough limbs,
the fine tales you cocooned yourself in.

You'd done that before, checking on me
from time to time, keeping me tethered,
in the doldrums I couldn't shake off

without help. Okay, I admit I was
between a blank canvas and a fresco
that needs repair—what to do first?

Take another tumble down the rabbit hole
or untether myself from you? Certain
I should go. Not go. Go.

Bathing in heavenly light and

blind to our blindness,
that's the halo effect,
plain and simple—
the illusion

that because this man
you thought was only
yours, and because he
is gorgeous, everything
about him is better.

When I knit, the halo effect
is a little less complex,
doesn't require psychology:

Blend a luxurious combed yarn
with a strand of mohair
that swan-dives into it.

The mohair softens
an already sumptuous look,
makes it more tantalizing,
whispers *take me, wrap me*
around you.

It *is* nearly irresistible.
Who can ignore the effect
of this needlework?—

everything about it is more
than you could ever expect.
And it can't deceive you
like that man did.

If only this poem

could be you when we first
met in the yard of that snazzy bar
to sip beer in cold mugs, our knees
knocking against table legs.
The wind kicking up
to blow my hair into a wild mess.
Breezes carrying your voice up
into the crown of a huge live oak
so that I only heard words dripping
down as whispers.

If only I'd been more acquainted
with the night, like a Frost sonnet
and its perfectly timed rhythms,
its impeccably tuned rhymes.
Or if I'd been as eloquent as
the poet's blank verse, where *Earth's*
the right place for love, where
I'd not be afraid to climb the heights
of the birches, bending till I could
bear no more.

If only my children had been older,
could stay alone while I remained
out late, too late, or I'd been willing
to have the babysitter stay longer—or
that you could bring me to say *yes.*

If only the moment hadn't begun
after the discordant notes from
my soon-to-be ex, whose phone
attacks unsettled most of my nights,
dimming the lamps on my street—
maybe I'd have found my heart's
tempo, measured and lyric, to mend
the bruising hurt. I might've steadied
my breath, the sigh of its rise and fall,
and its rising again, relaxed into

the oxygen of a fresh metaphor,
the urgency of the unruly thyme
spreading unchecked in my garden,
and the lilacs opening along the walls
of the ruins I lived in then.

First, You Have to Know Darkness

Because a field is moving light,
it might let you
glimpse its brightness for a moment,
though you

want to watch at all hours
as the meadow shapes
and reshapes
itself in a fluid passion
of wild grasses, timothy,

clumps of goldenrod
that every spring,
plant
themselves, then flame
in late summer
like a houseful of candles,

attracting
blue and coppery butterflies,
garden snakes,
wasps, and you,
and seeks to hurt no one.

Two Raccoons at Night after Rain

So huge, these two,
glowing under
street-lights,
rain from a live oak
dripping on them
as they look up
at shimmering limbs.

Across the street,
I and my dog
take
the day’s last walk.

She sees them
first, stopping
to stare
as if their presence
has overwhelmed
her most basic instinct
to go after them.

When I notice,
I startle too.
Usually, there’s not
another soul
here at this hour.

Yet here are two, frozen
in wonder and surprise.

I want those feelings,
and have felt them—
a while back. How far?

Watching them,
my eyes follow theirs,
rise to the flickering

branches,
above

then down this
glittered lawn,
the washed road.

The Migratory Seasons

Golden plovers fly over open ocean,
for days, from Alaska to Hawaii,
no place to land along the way—

catnapping in flight,
in a slow-wave drowse,
this curious trick—

keeping one eye open,
one brain-hemisphere alert
while the other side drops into sleep,
the other eye closes down.

We humans can hardly approximate
this state—and only in our troubled rest—

one hemisphere slow-sleeps while
the other half-dreams in shallows
of a turgid river, going nowhere.

In such states, the body feels
so restless that by morning, we
scarcely feel like ourselves
and can't move easily into the day.

On good nights, sleep wants us
to discover an old friend we thought
we'd lost. Or take a deep-dive
into our interior rooms.

Or probe the possibilities
for a new relationship
a fresh start
a way to solve an old problem.

Not often, we feel an airy uplift
carrying us aloft—the start
of our own migratory season.

A Cold Blue Swirl

High clouds, winter-white cirrus,
scatter light over a frosted field.

Black baldies huddle
under a scant windbreak, creatures
dark as exhaustion, the field light

as my sleep, and bare as the trees,
just black trunks and branches.

Soon a snowstorm
and its swirling blue cold
will take over, the cattle gathering

with no storm-shed, no straw beds,
no sweet alfalfa, no manger to weather

what's to come. Such is the forecast,
such are my furrows of worry
for the black baldies, so docile.

Across the one-lane bridge, I pull over,
the only car here, and I watch the herd

turn their white faces, those bright beacons,
toward me. Their coal-black eyes search
mine, anticipating that I am not just

a passerby, but a watcher to keep watch,
a mother with an instinct to enfold, to hold.

I've crossed this bridge dozens of times,
not grasping that this ice-glittered field is
home to such devotion, and beseeching—

cows hovering over their winter-calves,
covering their young against raw winds.

The Claim

This morning, plums hang ripe
in the orchard, nearly ready to be
sugared and boiled down for jam.
The world is not such a bad place
after all. A look in the barn,
and the lamb born in the night
rests with its ewe.

The form of all things—
the plum-ness, the lamb-ness,
the impression in the hay—disclose
the body as home, the central nature
of being. This claim to existing
in the world.

Last night, the violet darkness
consumed our lanterns along the path—
time to lamb, even with so little light.
We called to the ewe, who turned
her face toward the door's sweeping draft.

How was it she bleated so softly
just then, when we saw her body convulse,
and later when there was new life?
Is it her nature to stay so quiet?—

to hide what we could hardly see,
the lamb lifting its open mouth to claim
its mother. Would she own her offspring?
And what if she refused? What is it,
never to be claimed?

After a beat, she let the lamb
latch on. And so they were
joined—lamb and ewe indulging
in a feast of intimacy as the darkness
gave way to the dull blue light of dawn.

There Was, and Is

I became a mother.
My life upended
the way the persistent rain today
has filled the watering can,
overturning it.

There is love seeking love,
always. My own mother held me
so close that I could feel her heart
beat alongside mine.

It is my mother's heart
that beats through me for
my own son and daughters—
my plangent link, the cord
that still pulses.

This doesn't mean not loving
you, Reader, or others, really.
The Greeks have seven words
for *Love.* Surely you know
Philia for friendship and *Eros*
for romantic passion.

What courses from my mother
to me to my children
is *Storge,* the unconditional
heartbeat for them, and *Pragma,*
committed and long-lasting.

Those feelings course and pool
and stream,
soaking their grounding
like today's rain drenches
the garden soil
to green the parsley
and flush the lavender.

Near Dusk

I've walked near dusk along the corn rows, down
by wheat's end, this river that divides the land.
I've gone too far alone. Quail rise to howling
from the opposite bank: coyotes. I know they
will track me and won't cross over yet.

In the east, clouds have built all day,
and are furtive, coming to these fields
where thin green stalks list and wheat stands
stunted. The clouds are like you that way.

I smell water in them, knowing when they open
they will soak everything. Their cool breath
stiffens the back of my neck, pours over and
in me when I turn to drink air in great gulps.
My palms climb to feel the silky breeze.

Wind skims my skirt, over hollows where
no more daughters or sons can come to us.
I know now not to ask for a change
in weather. It always arrives soon enough.

I want to call them back, the lost children,
the same way I would your voice. Too far
into the field, coyotes near, I turn back
for the house, for your voice that might yet
cross under the sills, along the dull panes.

South of Questa

South of Questa and Cristobal, a wind blows over
the skin of sand, through the piñons. A sound rises
like vowels from an open throat, singing. You want
to learn the words.

Without really meaning to, you drive the hills, a road
that yaws, to the Franciscan mission, a buttressed
adobe church where few tourists wander.

Simple white crosses ascend from each bell tower,
and between them, over the arched entry.

Inside a graying *abuela* lights two candles, drops
coins in the wooden box. You cannot hear her prayer
only her low voice. Like others, you are here
for remission.

You light a candle in memory of your old self, innocence
you hardly remember. You breathe words of prayer
not knowing if they will be sent up.

Faith is not a concept you often count on, though at night
you believe you hear the shofar's call to Canaan.

Today on the drive home, you watch the wet clouds swirl
in the distance north of Wheeler Peak, then a flock of sheep
and its bellwether grazing in sparse pasture several miles
off to the west.

A man once found gold in this land after all the talk
of Cibola died down. Though you may not be able to
name what is missing, what can't be found, or

even say what needs resolution, let it go for a while.
You want to get back to Questa before the storm.

Halfway There, and Scared

Walking after dusk, you get to know yourself.
The path to the cabin goes toward a night
so deep, that its purple and navy swim
in your field of vision. Bright pinpoints—
lightning bugs—weave and turn before you.
Halfway there, and scared, you swing the lantern.
That is your habit to create a narrow path
through the swell of night. It drives you
forward even when you can't see, and in fear.
There's the awful pleasure of walking to get there
and trying not to make too much of the dark—
you won't be defined so much by it, or old losses.
This place doesn't tell that story. Up ahead
the covered porch takes form in soft yellow light.
There, you'll swat away the moths lively in it.

Between Dawn and Day, What Distance

Always Steinbeck's dawn begins gray,
forms of the world silhouetted.
Its inhabitants, living
not on optimism but hope,
will see within an hour

a sky filtering all the colors
before settling on blue,
the landscape filling in with detail,
the distinct world emerging.

Disembodied voices of night
anchor themselves in light
to their familiar forms: flashing wings
of hawks, barking offspring of coyotes,
the tapping and hissing of work

in fields and on the roads—
the giant tractors, the earth-augers,
the threshing combines.

It is the gray coming out of black
that in morning finds you,
will not let go.

It lifts you again from pillowed sleep—
that netherworld—pulling you up,
ferrying you back across

to begin your second labor,
killing off the several-headed monster
that ran you from the field—
and afterwards, entreating the sister-rains
to take the dust into themselves

until it runs with their generous grief
and the machinery breaks down
rusting to its elements.

What could the seeds do then
but give you back your work as
you comb and caress the gentle mares,
polish the wreaths of their harnesses,
sharpen your plow.

Notes

"The Bell Founder Advises Me" is inspired by an article from the *New York Times,* "Their Bells Have Tolled for Centuries." The article profiles two brothers who run the Marinelli Pontifical Foundry. The Marinelli family has been producing bells for the Vatican since 1339, using an age-old process. About the art of crafting of a bell, Armando Marinelli says, "There is always some magic in the crafting of a bell" and "every bell has a different soul."

I wrote "Mirabilia, in the Garden" while thinking of the language and sentiments in the Song of Solomon. Also, in many biblical passages, offering water is symbolic and is an act of service. The beloved in this poem celebrates service and intimacy with her great love.

In 2018, the Metropolitan Museum of Art's exhibition "Heavenly Bodies: Fashion and the Catholic Imagination" was set up to "feature a dialogue between fashion and medieval art . . . to examine fashion's ongoing engagement with the devotional practices and traditions of Catholicism." To say that I was fascinated by what I saw is an understatement. That exhibit stayed in my imagination for over a year because of its provocative nature—the portrayal of male and female roles through ecclesiastical garments. My two poems "Roberto Capucci's *Angel d'Oro*" and "Madonna Wedding Ensemble" are a result of that visit to the Met.

"Bathing in heavenly light and" is a poetic look at the "halo effect," the bias that one physical or personality trait influences another. This is most often evidenced when someone who is good-looking is also perceived as being intelligent or having stellar leadership qualities. The halo effect can also be seen in our thinking that "good people do only good things and bad people are all bad," according to Daniel Kahneman in his book *Thinking Fast, Thinking Slow.*

About the Author

Rebecca A. Spears, author of *Brook the Divide* and *The Bright Obvious,* has poems, essays, and reviews included in *TriQuarterly, Narrative, The Orchards Poetry Journal, Barrow Street, Verse Daily,* and other journals and anthologies. *Brook the Divide* was shortlisted for Best First Book of Poetry (Texas Institute of Letters, 2020). Her work has also received Pushcart and Best of the Net nominations. Most recently, Spears has been awarded a Poetry Fellowship from Porches Writing Retreat (2024) and named Writer-in-Residence at Dairy Hollow House (2025).

www.ingramcontent.com/pod-product-compliance
Lightning Source LLC
LaVergne TN
LVHW090618110826
845146LV00001B/437

* 9 7 9 8 9 0 1 4 6 7 1 8 3 *